Born in 1996

by

Kerry Butters.

Born in 1996.

Millennium:	2nd millennium
Centuries:	19th century – **20th century** – 21st century
Decades:	1960s 1970s 1980s – **1990s** – 2000s 2010s 2020s
Years:	1993 1994 1995 – **1996** – 1997 1998 1999

1996 (MCMXCVI) was a leap year starting on Monday (dominical letter GF) of the Gregorian calendar, the 1996th year of the Common Era (CE) and *Anno Domini* (AD) designations, the 996th year of the 2nd millennium, the 96th year of the 20th century, and the 7th year of the 1990s decade.

1996 was designated as:

- International Year for the Eradication of Poverty

Contents

Events

January

- January 1 – Fahd of Saudi Arabia temporarily gives power to Crown Prince Abdullah, his legal successor, due to illness.
- January 3 – Motorola introduces the Motorola StarTAC Wearable Cellular Telephone, the world's smallest and lightest mobile phone to date.
- January 4 – Hosni Mubarak, the president of Egypt, appoints a new government in response to accusations of corruption in the parliamentary elections in late 1995.
- January 5 – Hamas operative Yahya Ayyash is assassinated by an Israeli Shabak-planted, bomb-laden cell phone.
- January 7 – One of the worst blizzards in American history hits the eastern states, killing more than 150 people. Philadelphia receives a record 30.7 inches (78 cm) of snowfall, New York City's public schools close for the first time in 18 years and the federal government in Washington, D.C. is closed for days.

- January 8 – A Zairean cargo plane crashes into a crowded market in the center of the capital Kinshasa, killing 300.
- January 9–January 20 – Serious fighting breaks out between Russian soldiers and rebel fighters in Chechnya.
- January 11 – Ryutaro Hashimoto, leader of the Liberal Democratic Party, becomes Prime Minister of Japan.
- January 13 – Italy's prime minister, Lamberto Dini, resigns after the failure of all-party talks to confirm him. New talks are initiated by president Oscar Luigi Scalfaro to form a new government.
- January 14 – Jorge Sampaio is elected president of Portugal.
- January 15 – Amber Hagerman, a 9-year-old American child victim and namesake for the AMBER Alert system, is murdered in Arlington, Texas.
- January 16 – President of Sierra Leone Valentine Strasser is deposed by the chief of defence, Julius Maada Bio. Bio promises to restore power following elections scheduled for February.
- January 19
    - The *North Cape* oil spill occurs as an engine fire forces the tugboat *Scandia* ashore on Moonstone Beach in South Kingstown, Rhode Island. The *North Cape* Barge is pulled along with it and leaks 820,000 gallons of home heating oil.
    - An Indonesian ferry sinks off the northern tip of Sumatra, drowning more than 100 people.
- January 20 – Yasser Arafat is re-elected president of the Palestinian Authority.

Yasser Arafat

- January 21 – France undertakes its last nuclear weapon test.
- January 22 – Andreas Papandreou, Prime Minister of Greece, resigns due to health problems; a new government forms under Costas Simitis.
- January 24 – Polish Premier Józef Oleksy resigns amid charges that he spied for Moscow. He is replaced by Włodzimierz Cimoszewicz.
- January 26 – Whitewater scandal: U.S. First Lady Hillary Clinton testifies before a grand jury.
- January 27 – Colonel Ibrahim Baré Maïnassara deposes the first democratically elected president of Niger, Mahamane Ousmane, in a military coup.
- January 29
  - President Jacques Chirac announces a "definitive end" to French nuclear testing.
  - Fire destroys La Fenice, Venice's opera house.
- January 30 – Irish National Liberation Army leader Gino Gallagher is killed in an internal feud.
- January 30–February 5 – Sarah Balabagan is caned in the United Arab Emirates.
- January 31

- Colombo Central Bank bombing: an explosives-filled truck rams into the gates of the Central Bank in Colombo, Sri Lanka, killing at least 86 and injuring 1,400.
- An explosion in Shaoyang, China kills 122 and injures over 400 when 10 short tons (9.1 t) of dynamite in an illegal explosives warehouse underneath an apartment building detonate.

February

- February 4 – The 6.6 Mw earthquake near Lijiang in southwest China kills up to 322 people, injures 17,000, and leaves three-hundred thousand homeless.
- February 6 – Birgenair Flight 301, on an unauthorised charter flight from the Caribbean to Germany, crashes into the Atlantic Ocean off the coast of the Dominican Republic, killing all 189 passengers and crew.
- February 7 – René Préval succeeds Jean-Bertrand Aristide as president of Haiti, in the first peaceful handover of power since the nation achieved independence.
- February 8 – An IRA ceasefire ends with the Docklands bombing in London's Canary Wharf District, killing 2 and causing over £85 million worth of damage.
- February 9 – The element copernicium is created by fusing a ^{208}Pb nucleus with a ^{70}Zn nucleus, forming ^{278}Cn. Given the placeholder name "ununbium", the element is not named until 2010.
- February 10

- Chess computer "Deep Blue" defeats world chess champion Garry Kasparov for the first time.
- Bosnian Serbs break off contact with the Bosnian government and with representatives of Ifor, the NATO localised force, in reaction to the arrest of several Bosnian Serb war criminals.
- February 14 – Violent clashes erupt between Filipino soldiers and Vietnamese boat people, as the Philippines government attempts to forcibly repatriate hundreds of Vietnamese asylum seekers.
- February 15
  - In southwest Wales, the oil tanker *Sea Empress* runs aground, spilling 73,000 tonnes (72,000 long tons; 80,000 short tons) of crude oil, killing many birds.
  - The U.S. Embassy in Athens, Greece, comes under mortar fire.
  - A Long March 3 rocket at the Xichang Satellite Launch Center in China crashes into a rural village after liftoff, killing as many as 50.
  - Begum Khaleda Zia is reelected as prime minister of Bangladesh. The country's second democratic election is marred by low voter turnout, due to several boycotts and pre-election violence, which result in at least 13 deaths.
  - The UK government publishes the Scott Report.

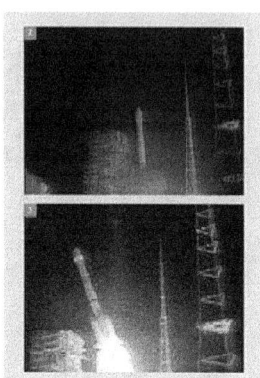

Feb.15: Long March rocket, with Intelsat 708 satellite, veers upon launch (images from Cox Commission report for U.S. Congress).

- February 17
    - In Philadelphia, Garry Kasparov beats "Deep Blue" in a second chess match.
    - The 8.2 Mw Biak earthquake shakes the Papua province of eastern Indonesia with a maximum Mercalli intensity of VIII (*Severe*). A large tsunami followed, leaving one-hundred sixty-six people dead or missing and 423 injured.
- February 18 – An IRA briefcase bomb in a bus kills the bomber and injures 9 in the West End of London.
- February 19 – A wooden ferry capsizes as it enters the port of Cadiz in the Philippines, killing 54 people.
- February 21 – King Fahd of Saudi Arabia announces his medical recovery in the national press and assumes power again from his brother, Crown Prince Abdullah.
- February 24 – Cuban fighter jets shoot down 2 American aircraft belonging to the Cuban exile group, Brothers to the

Rescue. Cuban officials assert that they invaded Cuban airspace.

- February 25 – Two suicide bombs in Israel kill 25 and injure 80; Hamas claims responsibility.
- February 27 – *Pokémon Red* and *Blue* are released in Japan by Nintendo as *Pocket Monsters: Red* and *Green*, the first role-playing video game in the Pokémon series, developed by Game Freak.
- February 28 – Canadian singer Alanis Morissette wins the top honor, Album of the Year award, at the 38th Annual Grammy Awards. At age 21, she is the youngest person to ever win this award, a record she will hold until 2010, when Taylor Swift wins.
- February 29
  - In Lumberton, North Carolina, Daniel Green is convicted of the murder of James Jordan, the father of basketball star Michael Jordan.
  - Faucett Flight 251 en route from Lima to Rodriguez Ballon airport crashes into a mountain near Arequipa; all 123 people on board are killed.
  - At least 81 people drown when a boat capsizes 120 kilometres east of Kampala, Uganda.
  - The Bosnian government declares the end of the Siege of Sarajevo.

March

- March 1 – Iraq disarmament crisis: Iraqi forces refuse UNSCOM inspection teams access to 5 sites designated for inspection. The teams enter the sites only after delays of up to 17 hours.

- March 2
  - Ranabima Royal College is established in Sri Lanka.
  - The Australian federal election, 1996 is held; Labor's Paul Keating loses to Liberal leader John Howard.
- March 3 – José María Aznar, leader of the Popular Party, is elected prime minister of Spain, replacing Felipe González.
- March 3–March 4 – Two more suicide bombs explode in Israel, killing 32. The Yahya Ayyash Units admit responsibility, and Palestinian president Yasser Arafat condemns the killings in a televised address. Israel warns of retaliation.
- March 6
  - Mesut Yılmaz, of ANAP forms the new government of Turkey (53rd government).
  - A boat carrying market traders capsizes outside Freetown harbour, in Sierra Leone, killing at least 86.
  - Chechen rebels attack the Russian government headquarters in Grozny; 70 Russian soldiers and policemen and 130 Chechen fighters are killed.
- March 8 – The People's Republic of China begins surface-to-surface missile testing and military exercises off Taiwanese coastal areas. The United States government condemns the act as provocation, and the Taiwanese government warns of retaliation.
- March 9 – Jorge Sampaio is the new Portuguese president.
- March 11 – John Howard is sworn in as the new Prime Minister of Australia.

- March 13 – Dunblane massacre: Unemployed former shopkeeper Thomas Hamilton walks into the Dunblane Primary School in Scotland and opens fire, killing 16 infant school pupils and one teacher before fatally shooting himself.
- March 14 – An international peace summit is held in Egypt, in response to escalating terrorist attacks in the Middle East.
- March 16 – Robert Mugabe is reelected president of Zimbabwe, although only 32 percent of the electorate actually voted.
- March 17 – Sri Lanka wins the Cricket World Cup by beating Australia in a disappointing final.
- March 18 – The Ozone Disco Club fire in Quezon City, Philippines kills 163.
- March 20 – The British government announces that Bovine spongiform encephalopathy has been likely transmitted to people.
- March 22 – Sweden's Finance Minister Göran Persson becomes his homeland's new Prime Minister.
- March 23 – The Republic of China (Taiwan) holds its first direct elections for president; Lee Teng-hui is re-elected.
- March 24
  - Islamists clash with security forces in Kashmir, killing 11.
  - The devastating Marcopper mining disaster on the island of Marinduque, Philippines takes place.
- March 25
  - An 81-day-long standoff begins between antigovernment Freemen and federal officers in Jordan, Montana.

- The 68th Academy Awards, hosted by Whoopi Goldberg, are held at the Dorothy Chandler Pavilion in Los Angeles with *Braveheart* winning Best Picture.
- March 26 – The International Monetary Fund approves a $10.2 billion loan to Russia for economic reform.
- March 28
  - Fire breaks out at the Pasar Anyar shopping centre in Bogor, West Java. The first death toll estimate is 78 until rescuers notice that 68 of them are mannequins.
  - Three British soldiers are found guilty of the manslaughter of Danish tour guide Louise Jensen in Cyprus. Allan Ford, Justin Fowler and Geoffrey Pernell receive life sentences for the September, 1994 rape/murder.

April

- April 1 – The Halifax Regional Municipality in Nova Scotia is created.
- April 3
  - A Boeing 737 military jet crashes into a mountain north of Dubrovnik, Croatia. All 35 people on board die, including United States Secretary of Commerce Ron Brown (see 1996 Croatia USAF CT-43 crash).
  - Suspected "Unabomber" Theodore Kaczynski is arrested at his Montana cabin.
  - Massacres of Hutus by Tutsis in Burundi take place, with more than 450 killed in a few days.

- April 6
  - Fighting breaks out in Monrovia, Liberia, between various rebel factions struggling for power in the country's interrupted civil war. Several foreign nationals leave the nation.
  - Major League Soccer kicks off in front of an overflow crowd of 31,683 packed in Spartan Stadium, to witness the historic first game. San Jose Clash forward Eric Wynalda scores the league's first goal in a 1–0 victory over D.C. United.
  - Turkish authorities begin Operation Hawk, an army offensive against rebels from the Kurdish Worker's Party in southeastern Turkey.
- April 9 – In a common statement, the European Union officially recognizes the Federal Republic of Yugoslavia.
- April 11
  - The Israeli government launches Operation Grapes of Wrath, consisting of massive attacks on Lebanon, in retaliation for prior terrorist attacks, and sparking off a violent series of retaliations.
  - At Düsseldorf International Airport, smouldering polystyrene evolves into a major fire, killing 17 people inside the terminal building.
- April 18
  - Qana Massacre: Over 100 Lebanese civilians are killed after Israel shells the United Nations compound in Qana.
  - In reaction to the Qana Massacre, an Islamist group in Egypt open fire on a hotel, killing 18 Greek tourists and injuring 17 others.

- April 21 – A general election in Italy proclaims a new center-left government headed by Romano Prodi, replacing Silvio Berlusconi.
- April 24 – At the urging of Yasser Arafat, the Palestine Liberation Organization drops its clause calling for the removal of Israel. The Israeli government responds by dropping a similar clause concerning the existence of Palestine.
- April 26 – A regional security treaty is signed by the "Shanghai Five".
- April 28
  - Port Arthur massacre: Martin Bryant kills 35 people at the Port Arthur, Tasmania tourist site, Australia.
  - A bomb explodes in Bhaiperu, Pakistan, killing more than 60 people.

May

- May – Iraq disarmament crisis: UNSCOM supervises the destruction of Al-Hakam, Iraq's main production facility of biological warfare agents.
- May 4 – A Sudanese Federal Airlines jet crashes on a domestic flight in a severe dust storm, while making an emergency landing 325 kilometres northeast of Khartoum, killing all 53 passengers and crew.
- May 8 – The Keck II telescope is dedicated in Hawaii.
- May 9
  - South Africa's National Party pulls out of the 2-year-old coalition government, and the African National Congress assumes full political control.

- Ugandan president Yoweri Museveni wins a landslide victory in the country's first direct presidential elections, securing 75% of the vote.
- May 10
    - 1996 Everest disaster: A sudden storm engulfs Mount Everest with several climbing teams high on the mountain, leaving 8 dead. By the end of the month, at least 4 other climbers die in the worst season of fatalities on the mountain to date.
    - The Australian government introduces a nationwide ban on the private possession of both automatic and semi-automatic rifles, in response to the Port Arthur massacre.
    - Vietnamese Vietnamese boat people in Hong Kong, facing forced repatriation due to their classification as economic migrants rather than refugees, stage a protest at the Whitehead Detention Centre.
- May 11 – After takeoff from Miami, a fire started by improperly handled oxygen canisters in the cargo hold of Atlanta-bound ValuJet Flight 592, causes the Douglas DC-9 to crash in the Florida Everglades, killing all 110 on board.
- May 13 – Severe thunderstorms and a tornado in Bangladesh kill 600.
- May 15 – Nine hostages held by the Free Papua Organization in Irian Jaya are rescued after an operation by the Indonesian military; 2 other hostages are later found dead.
- May 17–28 – Atal Bihari Vajpayee, leader of the Bharatiya Janata Party, is elected the new prime minister of India, replacing P. V. Narasimha Rao of the Indian National

Congress. However, the party does not receive an overall majority and Vajpayee resigns 13 days later rather than face a no confidence vote, and is replaced by the United Front, led Deve Gowda.

- May 18 – The X Prize Foundation launches the $10 million Ansari X Prize, which is won in 2004, by Burt Rutan's SpaceShipOne.
- May 20 – Gay rights – *Romer v. Evans*: The Supreme Court of the United States rules against a law that prevents any city, town or county in the state of Colorado from taking any legislative, executive, or judicial action to protect the rights of homosexuals.
- May 21
  - The *MV Bukoba* sinks in Tanzanian waters in Lake Victoria, killing nearly 1,000 in one of Africa's worst maritime disasters.
  - The Trappist Martyrs of Atlas are executed.
- May 23
  - Swede Göran Kropp reaches the Mount Everest summit alone without oxygen, after having bicycled there from Sweden.
  - Members of the Armed Islamic Group in Algeria kill 7 French Trappist monks, after talks with French government concerning the imprisonment of several GIA sympathisers break down.
- May 27 – First Chechnya War: Russian President Boris Yeltsin meets with Chechnyan rebels for the first time and negotiates a cease-fire in the war.
- May 28 – Albania's general election of May 26 is declared unfair by international monitors, and the ruling Democratic

Party under President Sali Berisha is charged by the Organization for Security and Co-operation in Europe with rigging the elections. Several hundred protestors gather in Tirana to demonstrate against the election result.

- May 30
    - The Likud Party, led by Benjamin Netanyahu, wins a narrow victory in the Israeli general election.
    - The Hoover Institution releases an optimistic report that global warming will probably reduce mortality in the United States and provide Americans with valuable benefits.
- May 31 – FIFA decides to give the FIFA World Cup 2002, the first World Cup in Asia, to Japan and South Korea, becoming the first World Cup with co-host countries in the history of the event.

June

- June – Iraq disarmament crisis: As Iraq continues to refuse inspectors access to a number of sites, the U.S. fails in its attempt to build support for military action against Iraq in the UN Security Council.
- June 1–June 3 – The Czech Republic's first general election ends inconclusively. Prime Minister Václav Klaus and his incumbent Civic Democratic Party emerge as the winners, but are unable to form a majority government. President Václav Havel refuses to invite Klaus to form a coalition.
- June 4 – The space rocket Ariane 5 explodes 40 seconds after takeoff in French Guiana. The project costs European governments 7.5 billion US dollars over 11 years.

- June 6 – Leighton W. Smith, Jr. resigns as NATO commander in the face of increasing criticism.
- June 7 – An IRA gang kills Detective Garda Jerry McCabe during a botched armed robbery in Adare, County Limerick.
- June 8
    - The 10th European Football Championship (UEFA Euro 96) begins in England.
    - Steffi Graf defeats Arantxa Sánchez Vicario in the longest ever women's final at the French Open, to win her 19th Grand Slam title.
- June 10 – Peace talks begin in Northern Ireland without Sinn Féin.
- June 11
    - An explosion in a São Paulo suburban shopping centre kills 44 and injures more than 100.
    - A peace convoy carrying Chechen separatist leaders and international diplomats is targeted by a series of remotely controlled land mines; 8 are killed.
- June 12 – In Philadelphia, a panel of federal judges blocks a law against indecency on the Internet. The panel says that the 1996 Communications Decency Act would infringe upon the free speech rights of adults.
- June 13 – An 81-day standoff between the Montana Freemen and FBI agents ends with their surrender in Montana.
- June 15 – In Manchester, UK, a massive IRA bomb injures over 200 people and devastates a large part of the city centre.
- June 19 – Boris Yeltsin emerges as the winner in Russia's first round of presidential elections.
- June 20 – Thousands of Megawati Sukarnoputri supporters clash with police in Jakarta, Indonesia.

- June 23
  - The Nintendo 64 video game system is released in Japan.
  - Archbishop Desmond Tutu is given an official farewell at his retirement service.
- June 25 – The Khobar Towers bombing in Saudi Arabia kills 19 U.S. servicemen.
- June 26 – Journalist Veronica Guerin is shot and killed in her car just outside Dublin.
- June 28
  - A new government is formed in Turkey, with Necmettin Erbakan of Refah Partisi becoming prime minister of the coalition government, and deputy and foreign minister Tansu Çiller of the True Path Party succeeding him after 2 years.
  - The Constitution of Ukraine is signed into law.
- June 29
  - The Prince's Trust concert is held in Hyde Park, London, and is attended by 150,000 people. The Who headlines the event in their first performance since 1989.
  - An explosion in a firecrackers factory in Sichuan Province, China kills at least 36 people and injures another 52.
- June 30
  - Costas Simitis is elected president of the Panhellenic Socialist Movement of Greece.
  - Bosnian Serb leader Radovan Karadžić relinquishes power to his deputy, Biljana Plavšić.

- Germany defeats the Czech Republic 2-1 after extra time in the final of the European Championships.

July

- July
  - Iraq disarmament crisis: U.N. Inspector Scott Ritter attempts to conduct surprise inspections on the Republican Guard facility at the airport, but is blocked by Iraqi officials.
  - The Prague Manifesto declares the principles of the Esperanto movement.
  - Confrontations occur in Northern Ireland between police and Orange Order protestors at Drumcree Church (see Drumcree conflict).
- July 1
  - The Northern Territory in Australia legalises voluntary euthanasia.
  - German orthography reform of 1996 agreed internationally.
- July 2 – In Los Angeles, Lyle and Erik Menendez are sentenced to life in prison without the possibility of parole.
- July 3 – Boris Yeltsin is reelected as President of Russia after the second round of elections.
- July 5 – Dolly the sheep, the first mammal to be successfully cloned from an adult cell, is born at the Roslin Institute in Midlothian, Scotland.
- July 8 – Martina Hingis becomes the youngest person in history (age 15 years and 282 days) to win at Wimbledon in the Ladies' Doubles event.

- July 10 – *Harriet the Spy*, the first movie made by Nickelodeon Movies, premieres in theaters.
- July 11 – Arrest warrants are issued for Bosnian Serb war criminals Radovan Karadžić and Ratko Mladić by the Russell Tribunal in The Hague.
- July 12 – Hurricane Bertha: made landfall in North Carolina as a Category 2 storm, causing $270 million in damage ($407 million in present-day terms) to the United States and its possessions and many indirect deaths.
- July 13 – A Republican Sinn Féin bomb explodes outside of a hotel in Enniskillen, Northern Ireland, disrupting a wedding reception and injuring 17 people.
- July 16 – An outbreak of E. coli food poisoning in Japan results in 6,000 children being ill, including two deaths, after a group of school children eat contaminated lunches.
- July 17
  - The Community of Portuguese Language Countries (Comunidade dos Países de Língua Portuguesa) is constituted.
  - Paris and Rome-bound TWA Flight 800 (Boeing 747) explodes off the coast of Long Island, New York, killing all 230 on board.
  - Joe Klein admits that he is "Anonymous", the author of Primary Colors.
- July 18 – Howard Hughes is sentenced to life imprisonment at Chester Crown Court for the rape and murder of 7-year-old Sophie Hook at Llandudno 12 months previously. The trial judge recommends that Hughes, 31, should never be released. However, the Home Secretary set his minimum

term at 50 years in 2002, meaning he is eligible for parole in 2046.

- July 19
  - An F3 tornado 5.5 miles (8.9 km) away from the Westminster, Maryland city center injures 3 people and causes $5 million in damages ($7.54 million in present-day terms).
  - The 1996 Summer Olympics in Atlanta, United States, begin.
  - Bosnian Serb President Radovan Karadžić resigns from public office in Republika Srpska after being indicted for war crimes.
- July 21 – The Saguenay Flood, one of Canada's most costly natural disasters, is caused by flooding on the Saguenay River in Quebec.
- July 24 – The Dehiwala train bombing kills 56 commuters outside Colombo.
- July 25 – The Tutsi-led Burundian army performs a coup and reinstalls previous president Pierre Buyoya, ousting current president Sylvestre Ntibantunganya.
- July 27 – The Centennial Olympic Park bombing at the 1996 Summer Olympics kills 1 and injures 111.
- July 29 – The child protection portion of the Communications Decency Act (1996) is struck down as too broad by a U.S. federal court.

August

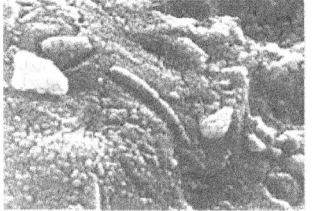

The electron microscope revealed chain structures in meteorite fragment ALH84001.

- August 1
  - Sarah Balabagan returns to the Philippines.
  - A pro-democracy demonstration supporting Megawati Sukarnoputri in Indonesia is broken up by riot police.
- August 4 – The 1996 Summer Olympics conclude.
- August 6
  - NASA announces that the Allan Hills 84001 meteorite, thought to originate from Mars, may contain evidence of primitive lifeforms.
  - The Australian census is conducted.
  - The American punk rock band the Ramones play their last show.
- August 7 – Heavy rains kill more than 80 campers near Huesca, Spain.
- August 9 – Boris Yeltsin is sworn in at the Kremlin for a second term as President of Russia.
- August 11 – The British rock band Oasis plays the biggest free-standing concert in UK history at Knebworth, Hertfordshire.

- August 13 – Data sent back by the Galileo space probe indicates there may be water on one of Jupiter's moons.
- August 14 – A rocket ignited during a fireworks display in Arequipa, Peru knocks down a high-tension power cable into a dense crowd, electrocuting 35 people.
- August 15 – Bob Dole is nominated for President of the United States, and Jack Kemp for Vice President, at the Republican National Convention in San Diego, California.
- August 16
  - Brookfield Zoo, Chicago. After a 3-year-old boy falls into the 20-foot (6.1 m) deep gorilla enclosure, Binti Jua, a female lowland gorilla sits with the injured boy until his rescue. Video of the ape's actions make her world famous.
  - After having spent 378 days in a Taliban prison, the crew of Russian Il-76TD manage to overpower their guards, board their aircraft and fly to freedom (see: 1995 Airstan incident).
- August 18 The *San Jose Mercury News* publishes Gary Webb's three-part series on the Reagan CIA's role in crack cocaine importation to fund the Contras.
- August 20 – A thousands-large protest in Seoul, calling for reunification with North Korea, is broken up by riot police.
- August 21
  - Former president of South Africa, F. W. de Klerk, makes an official apology for crimes committed under Apartheid to the Truth and Reconciliation Commission in Cape Town.
  - In Britain Queen Elizabeth II issues letters patent on divorced former wives of British princes, taking away

from the ex-wives the attribute and style of Royal Highness. With that Sarah, Duchess of York as well as Diana, Princess of Wales legally cease to be Royals, but they remain as non-royal Duchess and Princess. Still they are allowed to keep these titles for their children are in line to the throne.

- August 23 – Osama bin Laden writes "The Declaration of Jihad on the Americans Occupying the Country of the Two Sacred Places," a call for the removal of American military forces from Saudi Arabia.
- August 26
  - Chun Doo-hwan is sentenced to death, after being found guilty of mutiny and treason.
  - Bill Clinton signs welfare reform into law.
  - Iraqi expatriates seeking refuge hijack a Sudanese airliner en route from Khartoum to Amman.
- August 28 – Their Royal Highnesses, the Prince and Princess of Wales, are formally divorced at the High Court of Justice in London. Her Royal Highness The Princess of Wales is restyled Diana, Princess of Wales, due to the Queen's letters patent issued a week earlier.
- August 29
  - U.S. President Bill Clinton and Vice President Al Gore are renominated at the Democratic National Convention in Chicago.
  - A Russian Tupolev 154 jetliner crashes into a mountain as it approaches the airport at Spitsbergen, Norway, killing all 141 people on board.

- August 30 – The attempted raising of a 15-tonne section of the RMS *Titanic* fails, as 1,700 spectators, including survivors of the wreck, watch.
- August 31
  - Iraq disarmament crisis: Iraqi forces launch an offensive into the northern No-Fly Zone and capture Arbil.
  - The Big 12 Conference is inaugurated with a football game between Kansas State University and Texas Tech University in Manhattan, Kansas.

September

- September 2 – A permanent peace agreement is signed at the Malacañan Palace between the Government of the Philippines and the Moro National Liberation Front.
- September 3 – The U.S. launches Operation Desert Strike against Iraq in reaction to the attack on Arbil.
- September 4 – The Revolutionary Armed Forces of Colombia attack a military base in Guaviare, Colombia, starting 3 weeks of guerrilla warfare that will claim the lives of at least 130 Colombians.
- September 5 – Hurricane Fran makes landfall near Cape Fear, North Carolina as a Category 3 storm with 115 mph (185 km/h) sustained winds. Fran caused over $3 billion in damages ($4.53 billion in present-day terms) and killed 27 people, mainly in North Carolina. The name "Fran" was retired due to the extensive damage.

- September 10 – Comprehensive Nuclear Test Ban Treaty (CTBT) signed (it will be ratified 180 days after ratification by 44 Annex 2 countries).
- September 11 – Union Pacific finalizes its purchase of Southern Pacific that was effectively started almost a century before in 1901.
- September 12 - Ricardo López (stalker) sends a package, containing an acid bomb, to Icelandic singer Björk with the intention to kill or disfigure her, and then commits suicide. The package is intercepted by the Scotland Yard four days later, before doing any harm.
- September 13 – Alija Izetbegović is elected president of Bosnia and Herzegovina in the country's first election since the Bosnian War.
- September 18 – A North Korean Sang-O class submarine runs aground in South Korea. The crew are described as spies by the South Korean government and killed by the South Korean military.
- September 20 – Leader of Pakistani opposition party Pakistan Peoples Party Murtaza Bhutto is killed during a gun battle with police.
- September 20 – Tiger Cave Kiln discovered at Hangzhou in the Chinese province of Zhejiang.
- September 22 – The Panhellenic Socialist Movement under the leadership of Costas Simitis succeeds in the 1996 Greek legislative election.
- September 24 – U.S. President Bill Clinton signs the Comprehensive Nuclear-Test-Ban Treaty at the United Nations.

- September 25 – The last of the Magdalene asylums is closed in Ireland.
- September 27 – In Afghanistan, the Taliban capture the capital city of Kabul, after driving out President Burhanuddin Rabbani and executing former leader Mohammad Najibullah.
- September 30 – The United States Congress passes an amendment that bars anyone convicted of even misdemeanor level domestic violence from obtaining and possessing firearms.

October

- October 2
  - The Electronic Freedom of Information Act Amendments are signed by U.S. President Bill Clinton.
  - The former prime minister of Bulgaria, Andrey Lukanov, is assassinated.
  - An Aeroperú Boeing 757 crashes into the Pacific Ocean when the instruments fail just after takeoff from Lima Airport, killing all 70 on board.
- October 6 – The government of New Zealand agrees to pay $130 million worth of compensation for the loss of land suffered by the Māori population between the years of 1844 and 1864.
- October 7 – News Corporation launches the Fox News Channel as a 24-hour news channel to compete against CNN
- October 15 – Several large strikes begin in various industries across Belgium in protest to the dismissal of the magistrate Jean-Marc Connerotte by the Supreme Court.

- October 22 – A fire at La Planta prison in southwest Caracas, Venezuela, kills 30 prisoners.
- October 23 – The O. J. Simpson civil trial begins in Santa Monica, California.
- October 30 – Fighting erupts when Banyamulenga Tutsis of Laurent Kabila in Zaire seize Uvira and proceed to kill Hutu refugees.
- October 31 – A Brazilian TAM Fokker airliner crashes into a densely populated area of São Paulo, killing 103.

November

- November – Iraq disarmament crisis: UNSCOM inspectors uncover buried prohibited missile parts. Iraq refuses to allow UNSCOM teams to remove remnants of missile engines for analysis outside of the country.
- November 5
  - Pakistani prime minister Benazir Bhutto's government is dismissed by President Farooq Leghari after widespread allegations of corruption.
  - United States presidential election, 1996: Incumbent Democratic President Bill Clinton defeats his Republican challenger, Bob Dole.
- November 7
  - A devastating category 4 cyclone strikes Andhra Pradesh, India. The storm surge sweeps fishing villages out to sea, over 2,000 people die. 95 percent of the crops are completely destroyed.
  - NASA launches the Mars Global Surveyor.

- November 8 – All 141 people on board a Nigerian-owned Boeing 727 die when the aircraft crashes into the Atlantic Ocean while approaching Lagos airport.
- November 12 – Saudi Arabian Airlines Boeing 747 collides in mid-air with Kazakhstan Airlines Il-76 in New Delhi, India, resulting in the loss of 349 lives.
- November 15 – State Street in Chicago is re-opened to pedestrian traffic.
- November 16
  - Mother Teresa receives honorary U.S. citizenship.
  - The scoreboard at Buffalo's $127.5 million HSBC Arena falls to the ice just hours before a National Hockey League game; no one is injured.
- November 17
  - A bomb explosion in Kaspiysk, Russia, kills 32 people.
  - Emil Constantinescu is elected president of Romania.
- November 18
  - World-renowned bird expert Tony Silva is sentenced to 7 years in prison without parole, for leading an illegal parrot smuggling ring.
  - Frederick Chiluba is reelected president of Zambia.
- November 19
  - Martin Bryant is sentenced to 35 consecutive sentences of life imprisonment plus 1035 years without parole for murdering 35 people in a shooting spree in Tasmania earlier this year.
  - Preparatory Commission for the Comprehensive Nuclear Test Ban Organization (CTBTO) established.
  - *STS-80*: Space Shuttle Columbia conducts the longest mission of the Space Shuttle program.

- November 21
  - A propane explosion at the Humberto Vidal shoe store and office building in San Juan, Puerto Rico kills 33.
  - Demonstrators in Zagreb demand the survival of Radio 101.
- November 23
  - The Republic of Angola officially joins the World Trade Organization, as *Angola*.
  - Ethiopian Airlines Flight 961 is hijacked, then crashes into the Indian Ocean off the coast of Comoros after running out of fuel, killing 125.
- November 25
  - An ice storm strikes the U.S., killing 26 directly, hundreds more from accidents. A powerful windstorm blasts Florida; winds gust to 90 mph.
  - The U.S. stock market, especially the Dow Jones Industrial Average, gains at an incredibly fast pace following the 1996 Presidential election. It gains 10 days in a row during the month.
  - The APEC Summit opens in the Philippines.
- November 26 – The Sands Hotel in Las Vegas is imploded to make way for the Venetian Hotel.

December

- December 2
  - U.S. President Bill Clinton signs the Electronic Freedom of Information Act Amendments.
  - Widespread student pro-democracy protests are broken up in Burma.

- December 5 – Federal Reserve Board Chairman Alan Greenspan gives a speech in which he suggests that "irrational exuberance" may have "unduly escalated asset values".
- December 9 – Jerry Rawlings is reelected president of Ghana.
- December 11 – Tung Chee-hwa is appointed to become the new leader of Hong Kong after it reverts to Chinese rule in 1997.
- December 12 – Uday Hussein is seriously injured in an assassination attempt.
- December 13 – Kofi Annan is elected by the United Nations Security Council the next Secretary-General of the United Nations.
- December 17 – The Túpac Amaru Revolutionary Movement takes 72 hostages in the Japanese Embassy in Lima, Peru.
- December 18 – The *loi Carrez*, or Carrez law governing property transactions, is enacted in France
- December 20 – Steve Jobs' company NeXT is bought by Apple Computer, the company co-founded by Jobs.
- December 25 – Six-year-old JonBenét Ramsey is murdered in the basement of her parents' home in Boulder, Colorado.
- December 26 – The largest strike in South Korean history begins.
- December 27 – Taliban forces retake the strategic Bagram Air Base, which solidifies their buffer zone around Kabul.
- December 29 – Guatemala and the leaders of the Guatemalan National Revolutionary Unity sign a peace accord that ends the 36-year Guatemalan Civil War.
- December 30

- In the Indian state of Assam, a passenger train is bombed by Bodo separatists, killing 26.
- Proposed budget cuts by Benjamin Netanyahu spark protests from 250,000 workers, who shut down services across Israel.

- December 31
  - The Atchison, Topeka and Santa Fe Railway is merged with the Burlington Northern Railroad to form the BNSF Railway, making it one of the largest railroad mergers in U.S. history.
  - The Hacienda in Las Vegas is imploded to make way for the Mandalay Bay.

Date unknown

- The General Motors EV1, the first production electric car of the modern era, is launched and becomes available for lease.
- The invasive species Asian long-horned beetle is found in New York.

Births

January

Ella Henderson

- January 1 – Andreas Pereira, Brazilian footballer
- January 2
  - Dior Hall, American hurdler
  - Xiaoyu Yu, Chinese figure skater
- January 5 – Tyler Ulis, American basketball player
- January 6 – Kishan Shrikanth, Indian actor and director
- January 7 – Fu Yuanhui, Chinese swimmer
- January 10 – Anna Sztankovics, Hungarian swimmer
- January 11 – Leroy Sané, German footballer
- January 12 – Ella Henderson, British singer
- January 13
  - Aníta Hinriksdóttir, Icelandic middle-distance runner
  - Kamil Majchrzak, Polish tennis player
- January 15 – Dove Cameron, American actress
- January 16 – Anastasia Grishina, Russian artistic gymnast

- January 18 – Sarah Gilman, American actress
- January 22 – Joshua Ho-Sang, Canadian ice hockey player
- January 23 – Chachi Gonzales, American dancer
- January 26
  - Zakaria Bakkali, Belgian footballer
  - Tyger Drew-Honey, English actor
- January 31 – Joel Courtney, American actor

February

Sasha Pieterse

Sophie Turner

- February 1
  - Dionne Bromfield, English singer-songwriter and television personality
  - Gianluigi Quinzi, Italian tennis player
- February 5 – Zeng Siqi, Chinese artistic gymnast
- February 7
  - Mai Hagiwara, Japanese singer
  - Aaron Ekblad, Canadian ice hockey player
- February 9 – Jimmy Bennett, American actor
- February 11 – Jonathan Tah, German footballer
- February 17
  - Erika Fasana, Italian artistic gymnast
  - Sasha Pieterse, South African/American actress
- February 19 – Allen Alvarado, American actor
- February 21 – Sophie Turner, English actress
- February 24 – Cristian Imparato, Italian singer
- February 25 – Emel Dereli, Turkish shot putter

March

- March 1 – Ye Shiwen, Chinese swimmer
- March 4 – Timo Baumgartl, German footballer
- March 5
  - Taylor Marie Hill, American model/Victoria's Secret Angel
  - Emmanuel Mudiay, Congolese professional basketball player
- March 6

  - Taylor Marie Hill

Timo Werner, German footballer

- ○ Yan Han, Chinese figure skater
- March 8 – Emil Imre, Romanian-born Hungarian short track speed skater
- March 9 – Giorgio Minisini, Italian synchronized swimmer
- March 16 – Anna Ovcharova, Russian/Swiss figure skater
- March 18 – Madeline Carroll, American actress
- March 19 – Feodosiy Efremenkov, Russian figure skater
- March 23 – Lauri Kivari, Finnish freestyle skier
- March 26 – Kathryn Bernardo, Filipina actress
- March 27 – Rosabell Laurenti Sellers, Italian-American actress
- March 28 – Xie Siyi, Chinese diver

April

Loïc Nottet

Abigail Breslin

- April 2
  - Polina Agafonova, Russian figure skater
  - Matheus Santana, Brazilian swimmer
- April 4 – Austin Mahone, American singer
- April 8 – Lorna Fitzgerald, English actress
- April 10
  - Thanasi Kokkinakis, Australian tennis player
  - Loïc Nottet, Belgian singer
- April 12
  - Polina Korobeynikova, Russian figure skater
  - Elizaveta Kulichkova, Russian tennis player
- April 14 – Abigail Breslin, American actress
- April 21 – Tavi Gevinson, American fashion blogger
- April 22 – Wendy Sulca, Peruvian singer
- April 23 – Álex Márquez, Spanish motorcycle racer
- April 24 – Ashleigh Barty, Australian tennis player
- April 26 – Allisyn Ashley Arm, American actress

May

Birdy

- May 2 – Julian Brandt, German footballer
- May 3
  - Mary Cain, American middle-distance runner
  - Noah Munck, American actor
  - Alex Iwobi, Nigerian footballer player
- May 4 – Arielle Gold, American snowboarder
- May 5 – Britney Simpson, American figure skater
- May 6 – Dominic Scott Kay, American actor
- May 9 – Mary Mouser, American actress
- May 10 – Tyus Jones, American basketball player
- May 14 – Martin Garrix, Dutch DJ, composer, musician and producer
- May 15 – Birdy, English singer and songwriter
- May 17 – Ryan Ochoa, American actor
- May 19 – Lakshmi Menon, Indian film actress
- May 18 – Yuki Kadono, Japanese snowborder
- May 23 – Katharina Althaus, German ski jumper

June

Alen Halilović

- June 1 – Tom Holland, English actor
- June 3 – Han Tianyu, Chinese short track speed skater
- June 4 – Ruby Harrold, English artistic gymnast
- June 10 – Julian De La Celle, American actor
- June 11 – Hakeeb Adelakun, English footballer
- June 12 – Anna Margaret Collins, American singer, songwriter and actress
- June 13
  - Kingsley Coman, French footballer
  - Kodi Smit-McPhee, Australian actor
- June 15 – AURORA, Norwegian Pop Singer
- June 16 – Lily Zhang, American table tennis player
- June 18 – Alen Halilović, Croatian footballer
- June 19 – Larisa Iordache, Romanian artistic gymnast
- June 20 – Sam Bennett, Canadian ice hockey player
- June 22 – Kong Sangjeong, South Korean short track speed skater
- June 28 – Donna Vekić, Croatian tennis player

July

Blake Michael

- July 1 – Adelina Sotnikova, Russian figure skater
- July 3 – Kendji Girac, French singer
- July 5 – Risa Shoji, Japanese figure skater
- July 11
  - Alessia Cara, Canadian singer and songwriter
  - Andrija Živković, Serbian footballer
- July 12 – Moussa Dembélé, French footballer
- July 13 – Jena Irene, American singer
- July 18
  - Dzhamaldin Khodzhaniyazov, Russian footballer
  - Siebe Schrijvers, Belgian footballer
  - Yung Lean, Swedish rapper and record producer
- July 22
  - Skyler Gisondo, American actor
  - Jane Oineza, Filipina actress
- July 23
  - Danielle Bradbery, American singer
  - Rachel G. Fox, American actor
- July 30 – Fatin Shidqia, Indonesian singer
- July 31 – Blake Michael, American actor

August

Brianna Hildebrand

- August 1 – Cymphonique Miller, American actress and singer
- August 2 – Simone Manuel, American swimmer
- August 5 – Francesca Deagostini, Italian artistic gymnast
- August 7 – Liam James, Canadian actor
- August 10 – Jacob Latimore, American singer, actor and dancer
- August 13 – Antonia Lottner, German tennis player
- August 14
    - Brianna Hildebrand, American Actress
    - Neal Maupay, French footballer
- August 22 – Jessica-Jane Applegate, British Paralympic swimmer
- August 24 – Kenzo Shirai, Japanese gymnast
- August 27
    - Ebru Topçu, Turkish footballer
    - Wang Jianan, Chinese long jumper
- August 30

- Chen Dequan, Chinese short track speed skater
- Gabriel Barbosa, Brazilian footballer
- Trevor Jackson, American actor, writer, singer and dancer

September

Zendaya

- September 1 – Zendaya, American actress and singer
- September 5 – Richairo Živković, Dutch footballer
- September 9 – Jaïro Riedewald, Dutch footballer
- September 12 – Colin Ford, American teen actor and voice actor
- September 17 – Ella Purnell, English actress
- September 19 – Pia Mia, Guamanian singer-songwriter and model
- September 20 – Jerome Sinclair, English footballer
- September 23
  - Lee Hi, Korean singer
  - Evgeny Rylov, Russian swimmer
- September 25
  - Max Christiansen, German footballer

- ○ Mie Nielsen, Danish swimmer
- ○ Jake Pratt, English actor
- September 27 – Princess Iman bint Abdullah of Jordan

October

- October 3 – Kelechi Iheanacho, Nigerian footballer
- October 4 – Ryan Lee, American actor
- October 8 – Sara Takanashi, Japanese ski jumper
- October 9 – Bella Hadid, American model, Reality TV star
- October 10 – Oscar Zia, Swedish singer
- October 15 – Zelo, Korean singer (B.A.P)
- October 24 – Kyla Ross, American gymnast
- October 28
  - ○ Jasmine Jessica Anthony, American actress
  - ○ Lee June-hyoung, South Korean figure skater
- October 30 – Mizuki Fukumura, Japanese singer

November

Lorde

- November 3 – Aria Wallace, American actress

- November 4
  - Adelén, Norwegian-Spanish singer
  - Kaitlin Hawayek, American ice dancer
  - Michael Christian Martinez, Filipino figure skater
- November 7 – Lorde, New Zealand singer-songwriter
- November 9 – Nguyễn Thị Ánh Viên, Vietnamese swimmer
- November 11
  - Gianluca Gaudino, German footballer
  - Tye Sheridan, American actor
- November 13 – Hiba Nawab, Indian television actress
- November 14 – Borna Ćorić, Croatian tennis player
- November 17 – Ruth Jebet, Kenyan-born Bahraini long-distance runner
- November 18 – Noah Ringer, American actor
- November 19 – Liliána Szilágyi, Hungarian swimmer
- November 22 – Madison Davenport, American actress and singer
- November 23
  - Lia Marie Johnson, American actress and Internet personality
  - Anna Yanovskaya, Russian ice dancer
- November 26 – Louane Emera, French singer and actress
- November 27 – Hailey Baldwin, American model and socialite

December

Hailee Steinfeld

- December 4 – Daria Svatkovskaya, Russian artistic gymnast
- December 6 – Stefanie Scott, American actress
- December 10 – Jérémy Gabriel, French Canadian singer
- December 11
  - Jack Griffo, American actor
  - Hailee Steinfeld, American actress, model and singer
- December 14 – Li Zijun, Chinese figure skater
- December 17 – Elizaveta Tuktamysheva, Russian figure skater
- December 21
  - Atanas Kolev, Bulgarian basketball player, rapper
  - Kaitlyn Dever, American actress
- December 28 – Alfred Kipketer, Kenyan middle-distance runner
- December 29 – Dylan Minnette, American actor

Deaths

January

Arleigh Burke

François Mitterrand

- January 1
    - Malladihalli Sri Raghavendra Swamiji, founder of Anatha Sevashrama Trust, Malladihalli (b. 1890)
    - Moshe Aryeh Freund, Chief Rabbi (av beis din) of the Edah HaChareidis in Jerusalem (b. 1894)
    - Arleigh Burke, U.S Navy Admiral and Chief of Naval Operations (b. 1901)
    - Arthur Rudolph, German rocket engineer (b. 1906)
- January 2 – Karl Targownik, Hungarian psychiatrist and Holocaust survivor (b. 1915)

- January 5
  - Yahya Ayyash, Palestinian shaheed (b. 1966)
  - Lincoln Kirstein, American writer and impresario (b. 1907)
  - Richard Versalle, American operatic tenor (b. 1932)
- January 7 – Tarō Okamoto, Japanese artist (b. 1911)
- January 8 – François Mitterrand, President of France (b. 1916)
- January 9
  - Fearless Nadia, Indian actress and stuntwoman (b. 1908)
  - Sultan Rahi, Pakistani film actor (b. 1938)
- January 11
  - Harold Walter Bailey, English scholar of Khotanese, Sanskrit, and the comparative study of Iranian languages (b. 1899)
  - Eric Hebborn, art forger (b. 1934)
- January 15
  - Les Baxter, American musician and composer (b. 1922)
  - Paramount Chief Moshoeshoe II of Lesotho (b. 1938)
- January 17 – Barbara Jordan, American politician (b. 1936)
- January 18
  - Leonor Fini, Argentine artist (b. 1908)
  - Endel Puusepp, Soviet Estonian World War II pilot (b. 1909)
  - Nandamuri Taraka Rama Rao, Indian (Telugu) film actor (b. 1923)
  - Rudolf Wanderone, American pocket billiards player also known as Minnesota Fats (b. 1913)
  -

- January 19
    - A. G. Gaston, American businessman (b. 1892)
    - Don Simpson, American film producer (b. 1943)
- January 20 – Gerry Mulligan, American musician (b. 1927)
- January 25 – Jonathan Larson, American composer and playwright (b. 1960)
- January 26 – Georg Alexander, Duke of Mecklenburg, head of the House of Mecklenburg-Strelitz (b. 1921)
- January 28
    - Joseph Brodsky, Russian-born poet, Nobel Prize laureate (b. 1940)
    - Jerry Siegel, American cartoonist (b. 1914)
- January 31 – Gustave Solomon, American mathematician and engineer (b. 1930)

February

Gene Kelly

Martin Balsam

Audrey Munson

- February 2
  - Fred S. Keller, pioneer in experimental psychology (b. 1899)
  - Gene Kelly, American actor and dancer (b. 1912)
- February 3 – Audrey Meadows, American actress (b. 1926)
- February 6 – Guy Madison, American actor (b. 1922)
- February 7 – Boris Alexandrovich Tchaikovsky, Russian composer (b. 1925)
- February 9
  - Adolf Galland, German general and World War II fighter ace (b. 1912)
  - Albert Jean Amateau, Turkish rabbi, businessman, lawyer and social activist (b. 1889)
- February 11
  - Kebby Musokotwane, Prime Minister of Zambia (b. 1946)
  - Cyril Poole, English cricketer (b. 1921)
  - Phil Regan, American actor (b. 1906)
  - Amelia Rosselli, Italian poet (b. 1930)

- February 12
  - Bob Shaw, Irish science fiction writer (b. 1931)
  - Ryōtarō Shiba, Japanese novelist (b. 1923)
- February 13 – Martin Balsam, American actor (b. 1919)
- February 14
  - Eva Hart, British survivor of RMS *Titanic* (b. 1905)
  - Hong Il Kim, Korean shooting victim (b. 1968)
  - Bob Paisley, English football manager (b. 1919)
- February 15
  - Tommy Rettig, American actor (b. 1941)
  - McLean Stevenson, American actor (b. 1929)
- February 16
  - Roger Bowen, American actor (b. 1932)
  - Pat Brown, Governor of California (b. 1905)
  - Brownie McGhee, American musician (b. 1915)
- February 17 – Evelyn Laye, British actress (b. 1900)
- February 20
  - Audrey Munson, American artist's model and film actress (b. 1891)
  - Tōru Takemitsu, Japanese composer (b. 1930)
- February 21 – Morton Gould, American musician and composer (b. 1913)
- February 23 – Helmut Schön, German football player and manager (b. 1915)
- February 25 – Haing S. Ngor, Cambodian actor (b. 1940)
- February 26 – Mieczysław Weinberg, Polish composer (b. 1919)
- February 27
  - Sarah Palfrey Cooke, American tennis player (b. 1912)
  - Pat Smythe, British showjumper and author (b. 1928)

March

Olga Rudge

Edmund Muskie

- March 2 – Lyle Talbot, American actor (b. 1902)
- March 3 – Marguerite Duras, French author and director (b. 1914)
- March 4 – Minnie Pearl, American comedian (b. 1912)
- March 5 – Whit Bissell, American actor (b. 1909)
- March 9 – George Burns, American actor and singer (b. 1896)
- March 10
    - Ross Hunter, American film producer (b. 1926)
    - Butch Laswell, American motorcycle stunt rider (b. 1958)
- March 11 – Vince Edwards, American actor (b. 1928)
- March 13 – Krzysztof Kieślowski, Polish film director (b. 1941)

- March 15 – Olga Rudge, American violinist (b. 1895)
- March 17
  - René Clément, French film director (b. 1913)
  - Elsa Respighi, Italian composer (b. 1894)
- March 18 – Odysseas Elytis, Greek writer, Nobel Prize laureate (b. 1911)
- March 19
  - Virginia Henderson, nurse, researcher, theorist and author (b. 1897)
  - Chen Jingrun, Chinese mathematician (b. 1933)
- March 25 – John Snagge, British radio personality (b. 1904)
- March 26
  - Edmund Muskie, American politician (b. 1914)
  - David Packard, American engineer (b. 1912)
- March 29 – Frank Daniel, Czech-born writer, director, producer, teacher (b. 1926)
- March 31 – Jeffrey Lee Pierce, American musician (b. 1958)

April

Greer Garson

P. L. Travers

- April 3
    - Herk Harvey, American film director (b. 1924)
    - Carl Stokes, American politician (b. 1927)
- April 4 – Barney Ewell, American athlete (b. 1918)
- April 6
    - John D. Bulkeley, U.S. Navy Vice Admiral, and Medal of Honor recipient (b. 1911)
    - Greer Garson, British-born American actress (b. 1904)
- April 7– Colleen Clifford, British-born Australian actress (b. 1898)
- April 8
    - George W. Jenkins, American businessman and founder of Publix (b. 1907)
    - Rush Limbaugh, Sr., American ambassador, lawyer, legislator, jurist and grandfather of Rush Limbaugh (b. 1891)
- April 11 – Jessica Dubroff plane crash while attempting to be the youngest person to fly across the United States (b. 1988)
- April 12 – Fred Alexander (historian), Australian historian (b. 1899)

- April 16 – Lucille Bremer, American actress and dancer (b. 1917)
- April 18 – Ronald Davies, American judge (b. 1904)
- April 20 – Christopher Robin Milne, English author and bookseller (b. 1920)
- April 21 – Dzhokhar Dudayev, Soviet-born Chechen politician and President of Ichkeria (1991–1996) (b. 1944)
- April 22 – Erma Bombeck, American humorist and writer (b. 1927)
- April 23 – P. L. Travers, Australian-born British actress, journalist, novelist and writer (b. 1899)
- April 25 – Saul Bass, American graphic designer (b. 1920)
- April 26
  - Milt Gaston, American baseball player (b. 1896)
  - Stirling Silliphant, American screenwriter and producer (b. 1918)
- April 28 – T. H. Clark, Canadian geologist (b. 1893)

May

Timothy Leary

- May 2 – Queen Mother Moore, African-American civil rights leader and a black nationalist (b. 1898)
- May 3 – Jack Weston, American actor (b. 1924)

- May 11
  - Nnamdi Azikiwe, President of Nigeria (b. 1904)
  - Rob Hall, New Zealand mountaineer (b. 1961)
- May 15
  - Charles B. Fulton, American judge (b. 1910)
  - Virgil Ross, American animator (b. 1907)
- May 17 – Scott Brayton, American race car driver (b. 1959)
- May 19 – John Beradino, American baseball player and actor (b. 1917)
- May 20 – Jon Pertwee, British actor (b. 1919)
- May 21
  - Paul Delph, American musician and producer (b. 1957)
  - Lash LaRue, American actor (b. 1917)
- May 22 – Seymour H. Knox III, hockey team owner (b. 1926)
- May 24
  - Jacob Druckman, American composer (b. 1928)
  - Joseph Mitchell, American writer (b. 1908)
  - Enrique Álvarez Félix, Mexican actor (b. 1934)
- May 25 – Bradley Nowell, American musician (b. 1968)
- May 29 – Tamara Toumanova, Russian dancer and actress (b. 1919)
- May 31 – Timothy Leary, American writer, psychologist, and advocate of psychedelic drug research and use (b. 1920)

June

Ella Fitzgerald

- June 1 – Neelam Sanjiva Reddy, Indian statesman, 6th President of India (b. 1913)
- June 2
    - John Alton, American cinematographer (b. 1901)
    - Ray Combs, American game show host, and comedian (b. 1956)
    - Leon Garfield, English children's author (b. 1921)
    - Pilar Lorengar, Spanish soprano (b. 1928)
- June 3 – Peter Glenville, English film director (b. 1913)
- June 5 – Vito Scotti, American character actor (b. 1918)
- June 6
    - Kusuo Kitamura, Japanese Olympic swimmer (b. 1917)
    - George Davis Snell, American geneticist, recipient of the Nobel Prize in Physiology or Medicine (b. 1903)
    - Merle Curti, leading American historian (b. 1897)
- June 10
    - Marie-Louise von Motesiczky, Austrian painter (b. 1906)
    - Jo Van Fleet, American actress (b. 1914)
- June 11

- Brigitte Helm, German actress (b. 1908)
- June 15 – Ella Fitzgerald, American singer (b. 1917)
- June 16 – Mel Allen, American sportscaster (b. 1913)
- June 19
  - G. David Schine, American businessman (b. 1927)
  - Edvin Wide, Swedish middle-distance and long-distance runner (b. 1896)
  - Hillevi Rombin, Miss Universe 1955 (b. 1933)
- June 23 – Andreas Papandreou, Prime Minister of Greece (b. 1919)
- June 26 – Veronica Guerin, Irish journalist (b. 1958)
- June 27 – Albert R. Broccoli, American film producer (b. 1909)

July

Claudette Colbert

- July 1
  - William T. Cahill, American politician (b. 1912)
  - Margaux Hemingway, American fashion model and actress (b. 1954)
- July 3 – Raaj Kumar, Indian film actor (b. 1926)
- July 5 – Erik Wickberg, Salvation Army general (b. 1904)
- July 9 – Eno Raud, Estonian children's writer (b. 1928)

- July 12
  - John Chancellor, American journalist (b. 1927)
  - Jonathan Melvoin, American musician (b. 1961)
- July 13 – Pandro S. Berman, American film producer (b. 1905)
- July 14 – Jeff Krosnoff, American race car driver (b. 1964)
- July 15 – Dana Hill, American actress (b. 1964)
- July 16 – John Panozzo, American drummer (b. 1948)
- July 17 – Paul Touvier, French collaborator with the Nazis in Occupied France during World War II, first Frenchman convicted of crimes against humanity (b. 1915)
- July 20
  - Stuart Clarence Graham, Australian army general (b. 1920)
  - František Plánička, Czech footballer (b. 1904)
- July 21 – Herb Edelman, American actor (b. 1933)
- July 22 – Jessica Mitford, Anglo-American author, journalist and political campaigner (b. 1917)
- July 23 – Aliki Vougiouklaki, Greek actress (b. 1933)
- July 25 – Howard Vernom, Swiss actor (b. 1914)
- July 28 – Roger Tory Peterson, American naturalist and artist (b. 1908)
- July 30
  - Claudette Colbert, American actress (b. 1903)
  - Arihiro Hase, Japanese actor and voice actor (b. 1965)

August

Tadeusz Reichstein

- August 1 – Tadeusz Reichstein, Polish-born chemist, recipient of the Nobel Prize in Physiology or Medicine (b. 1897)
- August 2 – Obdulio Varela, Uruguayan footballer (b. 1917)
- August 8 – Nevill Francis Mott, English physicist, Nobel Prize laureate (b. 1905)
- August 11
    - Rafael Kubelík, Czech-born conductor (b. 1914)
    - Vanga, Bulgarian prophet, mystic, clairvoyant and herbalist (b. 1911)
- August 12 – Viktor Hambardzumyan, Soviet Armenian scientist (b. 1908)
- August 13 – David Tudor, American pianist and composer (b. 1926)
- August 14 – Camilla Horn, German actress (b. 1903)
- August 18 – Geoffrey Dearmer, British poet (b. 1893)
- August 20 – Rio Reiser, German rock musician and singer (b. 1950)
- August 27 – Greg Morris, American actor (b. 1933)

September

Spiro Agnew

Paul Erdős

Dorothy Lamour

- September 1
  - Vagn Holmboe, Danish composer (b. 1909)
  - Karl Kehrle, Benedictine monk, beekeeper (b. 1898)
- September 5 – Isabel Wood Holt, wife of former Governor of West Virginia Homer A. Holt (b. 1899)
- September 7

- Bibi Besch, Austrian-American actress (b. 1940)
- Arda Bowser, professional football player (b. 1899)
- September 8 – Eyre de Lanux, American artist, writer, and art deco designer (b. 1894)
- September 9 – Bill Monroe, American "father of bluegrass" music (b. 1911)
- September 10
  - Joanne Dru, American actress (b. 1922)
  - Hans List, Austrian inventor and automotive pioneer (b. 1896)
  - Juanita Wright, WWE wrestling figure (b. 1934)
- September 11 – Deane Waldo Malott, American academic and administrator (b. 1898)
- September 12 – Ernesto Geisel, Brazilian general and statesman, former President of the Republic (b. 1907)
- September 13 – Tupac Shakur, American rapper and actor also known as "2Pac", "Makaveli" (b. 1971)
- September 14
  - Helen Cohan, American stage dancer and film actress, daughter of George M. Cohan (b. 1910)
  - Juliet Prowse, American dancer and actress (b. 1936)
- September 16 – Gene Nelson, American dance and actor (b. 1920)
- September 17 – Spiro Agnew, American politician, 39th Vice President of the United States (b. 1918)
- September 18 – Annabella, French actress (b. 1907)
- September 20
  - Paul Erdős, Hungarian mathematician (b. 1913)
  - Max Manus, Norwegian resistance fighter during World War II (b. 1914)

- September 21
    - Henri Nouwen, Dutch Catholic priest and author (b. 1932)
    - Sabine Zlatin, Polish-born French Resistance member (b. 1907)
- September 22 – Dorothy Lamour, American actress (b. 1914)
- September 23 - Fujiko F. Fujio, Japanese cartoonist (b. 1933)
- September 26 – Nicu Ceaușescu, son of Romanian leader Nicolae Ceaușescu (b. 1951)
- September 28
    - Mohammad Najibullah, former President of Afghanistan (b. 1947)
    - Geoffrey Wilkinson, English chemist, Nobel Prize laureate (b. 1926)
- September 29 – Leslie Crowther, British TV comedian and game show host (b. 1933)

October

Morey Amsterdam

- October 1 – Pat McGeown, Provisional Irish Republican Army member (b. 1956)
- October 4 – Silvio Piola, Italian footballer (b. 1913)

- October 5 – Seymour Cray, American computer scientist (b. 1925)
- October 6 – Ted Bessell, American actor (b. 1935)
- October 8 – Mignon G. Eberhart, American author of mystery novels (b. 1899)
- October 11 – Renato Russo, Brazilian singer, leader of Legião Urbana Brazilian rock band. (b. 1960)
- October 12 – René Lacoste, French tennis champion (b. 1904)
- October 13 – Henri Nannen, German journalist (b. 1913)
- October 13 – Beryl Reid, British actress (b. 1919)
- October 14 – Laura La Plante, American actress (b. 1904)
- October 16 – Jason Bernard, American actor (b. 1938)
- October 20 – J. Bracken Lee, American Politician (b. 1899)
- October 24
  - Artur Axmann, Nazi German Hitler Youth leader (b. 1913)
  - George P. Oslin, reporter, executive at Western Union (b. 1899)
- October 28 – Morey Amsterdam, American actor and comedian (b. 1908)
- October 30 – Eleanor Lansing Dulles, author, professor, and United States Government employee (b. 1895)
- October 31 – Marcel Carné, French film director (b. 1909)

November

Jean-Bédel Bokassa

Tiny Tim

- November 1 – Junius Richard Jayewardene, former President of Sri Lanka (b. 1906)
- November 2 – Eva Cassidy, American vocalist (b. 1963)
- November 3
    - Abdullah Çatlı, Turkish nationalist (b. 1956)
    - Jean-Bédel Bokassa of Central African Republic/Empire (b. 1921)

- November 5 – Eddie Harris, American Jazz musician (b. 1934)
- November 10
  - Imam Alimsultanov, Chechen bard (b. 1957)
  - Yafeu Fula (aka Yaki Kadafi), rapper from Tupac Shakur's group Outlawz (b. 1977)
- November 15 – Alger Hiss, American State Department official (b. 1904)
- November 16 – Loretta Alvarez, Pascua Yaqui midwife from the 1920s until the 1970s (b. 1892)
- November 17 – Sven Hörstadius, Swedish embryologist (b. 1898)
- November 18 – Zinovy Gerdt, Russian actor (b. 1916)
- November 20 – Franciszek Strynkiewicz, Polish sculptor (b. 1893)
- November 21
  - Abdus Salam, Pakistani physicist, Nobel Prize laureate (b. 1926)
  - Gail Stanton, Playboy centerfold June 1978 (b. 1954)
- November 22
  - María Casares, French-Spanish actress (b. 1922)
  - Mark Lenard, American actor (b. 1924)
- November 26 – Paul Rand, American graphic designer (b. 1914)
- November 27 – Gertrude Blanch, American mathematician (b. 1897)
- November 28 – Don McNeill, American tennis champion (b. 1918)
- November 30 – Tiny Tim, American musician (b. 1932)

December

Marcello Mastroianni

Carl Sagan

- December 3 – Babrak Karmal, President of Afghanistan (b. 1929)
- December 6 – Pete Rozelle, American commissioner of the National Football League (b. 1926)
- December 8 – Howard Rollins, American actor (b. 1950)
- December 9
  - Mary Leakey, British archaeologist (b. 1913)
  - Diana Morgan, British playwright and screenwriter (b. 1908)
  - James Basil Wilkie Roberton, New Zealand soldier, doctor, historian and writer (b. 1896)
- December 10 – Faron Young, American singer (b. 1932)

- December 11 – Willie Rushton, English comedian, actor, and cartoonist (b. 1937)
- December 13
  - Edward Blishen, English author (b. 1920)
  - Clarence Wijewardena, Sri Lankan musician (b. 1943)
- December 16 – Quentin Bell, English biographer and art historian (b. 1910)
- December 17 – Stanko Todorov, Bulgarian communist politician (b. 1920)
- December 18 – Irving Caesar, American lyricist (b. 1895)
- December 19 – Marcello Mastroianni, Italian actor (b. 1924)
- December 20 – Carl Sagan, American astronomer (b. 1934)
- December 21 – Margret Rey, American children's author and illustrator (b. 1906)
- December 29 – Mireille Hartuch, French singer (b. 1906)
- December 30
  - Lew Ayres, American actor (b. 1908)
  - Jack Nance, American actor (b. 1943)

Nobel Prizes

- Physics – David M. Lee, Douglas D. Osheroff, Robert C. Richardson
- Chemistry – Robert Curl, Sir Harold Kroto, Richard Smalley
- Medicine – Peter C. Doherty, Rolf M. Zinkernagel
- Literature – Wisława Szymborska
- Peace – Carlos Filipe Ximenes Belo and José Ramos-Horta
- Bank of Sweden Prize in Economic Sciences in Memory of Alfred Nobel – James Mirrlees, William Vickrey

In the News

The OJ Simpson trial begins when OJ is charged with murder.

Best Picture of the 68th Academy Awards is won by the film Braveheart.

The birth of the first successfully cloned mammal from an adult cell, Dolly the sheep.

The youngest person ever to win the Ladies' Doubles event at Wimbledon is Martina Hingis age 15.

Prince Charles and Diana, Princess of Wales get divorced.

Mad Cow Disease hits Britain.

The Summer Olympics are held in Atlanta United States.

IBM's Deep Blue defeats Chess Champion Gary Kasparov for the first time.

Popular Films - Independence Day, Twister, Mission: Impossible, and Jerry Maguire.

DVD's Launched in Japan.

American Pathfinder launched on its 310 million mile mission to Mars.

Nintendo releases their newest gaming system the Nintendo 64.

The Ozone layer over the Arctic continues to be depleted.

1996 Calendar

January 1996

Sun	Mon	Tue	Wed	Thu	Fri	Sat
	1	2	3	4	5	6
7	8	9	10	11	12	13
14	15	16	17	18	19	20
21	22	23	24	25	26	27
28	29	30	31			

February 1996

Sun	Mon	Tue	Wed	Thu	Fri	Sat
				1	2	3
4	5	6	7	8	9	10
11	12	13	14	15	16	17
18	19	20	21	22	23	24
25	26	27	28	29		

March 1996

Sun	Mon	Tue	Wed	Thu	Fri	Sat
					1	2
3	4	5	6	7	8	9
10	11	12	13	14	15	16
17	18	19	20	21	22	23
24	25	26	27	28	29	30
31						

April 1996

Sun	Mon	Tue	Wed	Thu	Fri	Sat
	1	2	3	4	5	6
7	8	9	10	11	12	13
14	15	16	17	18	19	20
21	22	23	24	25	26	27
28	29	30				

May 1996

Sun	Mon	Tue	Wed	Thu	Fri	Sat
			1	2	3	4
5	6	7	8	9	10	11
12	13	14	15	16	17	18
19	20	21	22	23	24	25
26	27	28	29	30	31	

June 1996

Sun	Mon	Tue	Wed	Thu	Fri	Sat
						1
2	3	4	5	6	7	8
9	10	11	12	13	14	15
16	17	18	19	20	21	22
23	24	25	26	27	28	29
30						

July 1996

Sun	Mon	Tue	Wed	Thu	Fri	Sat
	1	2	3	4	5	6
7	8	9	10	11	12	13
14	15	16	17	18	19	20
21	22	23	24	25	26	27
28	29	30	31			

August 1996

Sun	Mon	Tue	Wed	Thu	Fri	Sat
				1	2	3
4	5	6	7	8	9	10
11	12	13	14	15	16	17
18	19	20	21	22	23	24
25	26	27	28	29	30	31

September 1996

Sun	Mon	Tue	Wed	Thu	Fri	Sat
1	2	3	4	5	6	7
8	9	10	11	12	13	14
15	16	17	18	19	20	21
22	23	24	25	26	27	28
29	30					

October 1996

Sun	Mon	Tue	Wed	Thu	Fri	Sat
		1	2	3	4	5
6	7	8	9	10	11	12
13	14	15	16	17	18	19
20	21	22	23	24	25	26
27	28	29	30	31		

November 1996

Sun	Mon	Tue	Wed	Thu	Fri	Sat
					1	2
3	4	5	6	7	8	9
10	11	12	13	14	15	16
17	18	19	20	21	22	23
24	25	26	27	28	29	30

December 1996

Sun	Mon	Tue	Wed	Thu	Fri	Sat
1	2	3	4	5	6	7
8	9	10	11	12	13	14
15	16	17	18	19	20	21
22	23	24	25	26	27	28
29	30	31				

www.ingramcontent.com/pod-product-compliance
Lightning Source LLC
Chambersburg PA
CBHW071237280526
45787CB00002B/962